INVITATION

INVITATION

ATHOL WILLIAMS

Poems

Also by Athol Williams

Poetry

WHISTLEBLOWING
FRAGILE
BUMPER CARS
TALKING TO A TREE*
HEAP OF STONES*

Non-fiction

DEEP COLLUSION: BAIN AND THE CAPTURE OF
SOUTH AFRICA
THE BOOK OF EDEN
PUSHING BOULDERS: OPPRESSED TO INSPIRED

Children's

A GIRL CALLED H
THE OAKY SERIES

*As AE Ballakisten

Invitation
Athol Williams

First published by Theart Press in 2017
This edition published in 2023
www.theartpressbooks.com
Copyright © Athol Williams
www.atholwilliams.com

ISBN: 978-0-620-76791-0
ISBN: 978-0-620-76792-7 (e-book)

Set in Adobe Jensen Pro and Fontin Sans
Page design and typesetting by Theart Press

For my wife, Taryn Lock

CONTENTS

FINDING

I walk where the land flows into the sea,
searching, a shell perhaps.

Across the waters the bull's eye squall dips
and dives to scoop up bassoons and timpani,
cymbals that come racing toward my feet.
I am met by a travelling choir, hands cupped,
filled with arias from alien shores that wash
over the white canvas awaiting my footprints.
I walk, impressionist colours in full voice
following my steps.

I came searching, a shell perhaps,
but I leave, music.

SPACE

We need so little –
bowing branches that breathe
retired leaves onto a patch of green,
an impressionist's concert
flanked by an untidy wall of free ivy,
a drama of rickety garden chairs
separated from a clumsy table that tickles
our imagination; blue and sunlight that
twirl and twist with curiosity to weave
their way into frame.

This is all we need – space,
to flip through the beauty and wonder
of our minds' picture books;
space, for our spirits to roam.

SECRET WAY

There is no path,
only footsteps,
and music.

My way is born as I walk.

There is a destination,
many destinations, home
to my dreams,
but no path leading
there;
this I create by my music,
by my walking,
taking the first steps,
calling the distant closer.

CATHEDRAL

At the end of the back row
I find rest.

I hear no sermon,
I see no ceremony.

I sit alone
with the carved stone
and polished marble
like a lone candle
whose flame dances
to silent music.

Here I am.

TAKING NOTICE OF TIME

Where do these days hide?
Days of soft orange-yellow skies,
of clear water rivers,
pensively, flowing by;
of fresh green, sparkling fresh trees
and grasses and tall grasses
and leaves perched upon branches
dancing in a mellow breeze
under an umbrella
of soft orange-yellow skies,
where there's time,
time, to
notice time, to
notice hours, to
notice minutes, to
think about seconds,
time
to take long, slow, passionate puffs on a cheap cigar.

Where do these days hide?
where beyond distance
is more distance,
where ancient hills
and new blossoms
combine in static delight,
where quiet is so quiet that
it commands your attention,
where your soul is at such peace
that it weeps,

a cleansing of the toxins
that accumulate in thick resins
and crowd out,
crowd out the tiny rays of light,
choke the whispers of fresh air,
for it's hard to breathe
when racing at the speed of noise.

Let me cuddle up here beside this rock
and rest my head
and breathe
and take notice of time
and hope that time
will take notice of me.

Published in *Heap of Stones*,
Theart Press, 2009

CHORAL TREES

The trees are silent this morning.
Last night they threw their voices
across the valley imitating a spring
and then a raging, rambling, rolling river.
Now they stand quietly, gently panting,
hushed whispers, like teenage boys
who ran amuck in a quiet village,
drunk on fresh air, high on hormones,
now catching their breath, smiling
mischievously among themselves,
plotting their next drama of noisy chaos
that will stir the valley to life in song.

AT HOME IN OXFORD

I move my desk toward the sunlight,
to see more; is this not why I came here?

Two large rectangular eyes pour light
onto my desk, and rare heat onto
my bed of springs, malicious springs
that complain loudly each night,
and stab their fingers into my back.
The toilet seat is broken, the shower
is too small for me to turn, my chair
hard and unfriendly. Still, I smile,
sitting at my dull desk, dreaming;
is this not why I came here?

In this kitchen, Oxford stew was born –
cabbage, mushrooms, onions;
here I started swallowing statins
to hold my heart together. In this garden
I awoke the memory of riding a bike,
awaking fountains in my soul. Here
I failed at growing chickpeas and celery,
but found success in papers and exams
and life-stories.

Another stop along the large ellipse;
I learned and laughed and loved here;
is this not why I came here,
is this not why we go anywhere?

TO BE HELD

I want to sink into the softness
of beauty – a yearning to be held
there, to be held. To be
a bright orange pollen grain
that rests in the quiet fort
of thick-walled white tulip petals.
Held there, swollen with music,
to one day erupt into the expanse,
to become new beauty.

I want to cleanse my world
by sinking into beauty, being held
there, and creating
more beauty, more life.

Rather than cover darkness,
I want to uncover light; rather
than tear down tents of weeds,
I want to build towers of tulips,
places of beauty, of rest.

But for now, all I want, is to sink
into the softness of beauty,
to be held there, to be held.

Published in *Voyages: An Anthology*
(Age UK), 2016

SLUG

I enjoy these visits. It sneaks in
under the back door, leaving
two-minded diamond footprints
across the black carpet
to let me know it is here.
It doesn't come for food
or drink or to puke any
particular news or gossip,
just a visit, a little 'pop in'
for a meandering chat
about this and that
like a good old friend, the kind
where time together matters
more than words.
And then it waves on out,
back into the night, leaving
me to scrub the carpet of its visit
before my wife gets home.

Published in *McGregor Poetry Anthology*
2017

NO NAME

they ask her name,
but all she can speak of is the texture of the ocean;
she tells of the blinding bliss that is just a curve away;
she knows left and right, on and off, up and away;
and she knows the sound that dreams make in our veins.

she can sing the colour of magic; but a name,
she does not speak of a name.

Inspired by an *Irma Gerber* painting

IRISES

I wonder
if anyone ever asked Monet why he
painted;

why did he paint?

I wonder
if he was compelled
by an inner overwhelming power
that flowed
into jumbled words
attached to tuneless songs
that he saw, distinctly
and so unscrambled beauty
with his brush
and his eye
for truth.

Sometimes we get lost in beauty
that leaves us breathless, with questions
dripping from our lips.

ONLY THE LISTENING

There is a destiny
that haunts you, in the dark
of your meandering.
Only the listening
see
the tiny luminous pebbles
that lead to the light.
In that light,
a choir,
sings the eternal song
but deformed of one voice;
on cue
you come to life,
but only if you've been listening.

Published in *Talking to a Tree: Poems of a
Fragile World*, Theart Press, 2011

A WALK WORTH WALKING

Dream
with your eyes open, see
your life as it is, and then look
further into what it could be. Then walk
into that picture, that scene, that joyful reality.

The walk may be testing,
but a dream worth dreaming
often finds joyful reality, along
a walk worth walking.

KINETIC WISDOM

'Speak of progress,'
the student urged the teacher.

'Only the unafraid know progress,'
the teacher started, 'it is like riding a bike,'
bringing a frown to the student's brow.
'The faster you pedal, the greater the possible injury
but the further you go. The afraid barely move,
never pick up speed. The afraid don't get hurt
but go nowhere. The unafraid risk great injury
but make great progress.'

'That assumes you have purpose,'
the student challenged the teacher,
'progress is an illusion without purpose.'

'To stay on the bike you must keep moving,'
the teacher replied,
'as it is with progress,
as it is with knowing your purpose.'

SIGN ALONG THE WAY

I dreamed that my left eye went shut,
couldn't open, so I could only see
through one eye, my right eye.
It caused me no distress though:
'Perhaps I don't need it,' I told myself –
a sense that I lost my eye in the course of being –
one thing closing
for another to open.

I WILL KEEP WALKING

Clouds will come, dark clouds, but I,
I will keep looking, keep looking
to the sun for light, for warmth, and I,
I will keep walking.

And when, even the sun is drowned
in melancholy and smothered by
the darkest clouds, I, I will find light
and warmth, the brightest light
and most embracing warmth,
within me.

And it will lift me, back to my feet,
back to my mountaintop; it will lift me
so high that even the clouds will find joy
and shed their darkness, to reveal
life's magnificence.

This is my vow, though clouds come, I,
I will keep walking.

Published in *Voyages: An Anthology (Age UK)*,
2016

IF TODAY IS MY LAST

If today is my last
then I'll sit at the kitchen table
with her,
to water-soaked cereal with cashews
and bananas cut into coins in my bowl
as we've done, to welcome every sun
in our time. I'll hold her hand and rub
her leg and stroke the hair from her face,
slurping black coffee from a blue mug,
striped like road lanes I've criss-crossed
all of my life, drunk with dreams.

I'll find a spot in the grass where tiny
rays of light roam free among whispers
of fresh air, and there I'll stop, to listen.
I'll listen for screams, hoping to hear
none, I'll listen for truth, knowing I'll
hear some. I'll rest my head on the oak,
hold a stone in my palm, and perhaps
try one last time to fly.

Later we'll have a mosaic of veggies
on our plates, laughing, recounting our
moments and pictures as we've done
at the farewell of every sun in our time.

I'll lock our gaze, just a little longer,
clasp her in my arms, just a little tighter
and throw open my heart, as I lay to rest.
And if it should be that I happen to wake
for one last midnight snack, I'll spread
just a little extra hummus on my toast.

DOUBLE HAPPINESS

I

Clouds come and I can't see her star
but it is always there.

I wander, lost, off my path of joy
but it too, is always there.

Then clouds pass and I can see her star
and find my path, never alone,
for she is always here.

II

In my dark room, I return;
I become unborn, floating alone,
in soft silence, feeling nothing
but her heartbeat
everywhere, all over. Here
colour finds me: an abundant forest
of singing leaves and dancing light.

III

I will not leave this world naked,
as they say; I will leave draped
in her music, her heartbeat dancing
through the leaves of my branches.

IN THE EARLY HOURS

I miss you most in the early hours, as I wake
to days upon which darkness prolongs its grip.
The dark folds back the blossoms that colour our balcony,
it muffles the song of the red-breasted cuckoo on our sill,
it places scales on the eyes of the squirrels so they fall
from their branches outside our window.
There's no melody of hot bread from the bakery downstairs,
upon which to pour honey. No newborn coffee brew
to melt the fog of a snoozing head. No warm embrace
to kickstart the journey from dream to day.

I awake to endless nights,
for there can be no morning
without the sun.

ACKNOWLEDGEMENT

Love is, she
who walks gladly, leaking pail in hand,
beside him, along an uncertain path
to his dreamed riches, riches that could
never fill her pail but will feed his flame,
that mystical fire from which he hopes
warmth might dance in the cold hours,
and a light might sing in the dark days,
if not for many then at least for her.
Blessed with such love, he bows to her,
humbled, grateful.

For Taryn
Published in the poet's *Master in Philosophy*
thesis at Oxford University, April 2017

EACH OTHER

Wrapped 'round a large white table, we sat
this morning, friends of thirty summers,
breathing to life forgotten tales of teenage
mischief, of who stole who's school lunch,
and who liberated homework from whose
school bag, and whether in fact I really did
hold a classmate over the first floor balcony
threatening to drop her. Bursts of laughter
and exclamations peppered the soft 80s
music that whispered in the background as
we drifted from then to now with accounts
of husbands, and children and jobs ... unfamiliar
talk by familiar voices and familiar faces that
carry time with distinction, circled there like
the long orbit that had taken us apart and
now brought us here, to this moment, dripping
sweet in the joy of having paused together,
to look briefly over our collective shoulder,
not to return to the teens we were but to
draw out the light from the dark of years and
to brighten its colour; to hold hands, and then
to carry on till our orbits intersect once more.

We are each other's histories, I smiled, each
other's stories, each other.

MY CUE

'Outside,' my brother's text message reads,
which is short for, 'I am outside your house,'
my cue to toss out the key from my first floor
window so that he can come upstairs to visit.

What he doesn't know is that I don't need
the text message, because when he's close,
the tree in my garden stretches out a branch
and taps excitedly on my window, its leaves
quivering in delight, and I swear I can hear
it exclaim: 'It's him, it's him!' *This* is my cue.
I can't explain this little miracle …

                    but it happens every time.

MOTHER'S ROUTINE

She's followed this routine for fifteen years;
dutifully, religiously, never erring. Today,
is the first time that I am invited along.

We weave through the short streets
of my childhood ghetto in her silver Toyota
with cowhide-patterned seats.
We all frowned at the seat covers but
they were her choice so they became
our choice. I see a bucket on the back seat
but I do not enquire. It is her routine,
I don't know the protocol, dare I speak?
She is quiet, so I get lost in my thoughts
as we enter Jakes Gerwel Drive, that road
that ends in the sea. Like a lost river
it slithers aimlessly, carrying rusted cars
and dented dreams, its banks littered with
patched shacks and fragile lives.
We're driving against the flow – salmon
trying to make our way home, but we don't
know home. At a stop, a crowd of children
emerge from the reeds to swarm our car,
begging. We have no flesh on our bones
to spare, so we stare straight ahead,
ignoring their pain, chewing on our own.

One sees nothing along Jakes Gerwel Drive
that you want to see. I imagine a tourist bus

coming down this road, and wonder what the
guide would say, 'And over there we have ...,
oh, over here is ..., and this is where ...' Nothing.
Nothing worth seeing. Even Satan closes his eyes
along this road. I close my eyes. Mother has
Cliff Richard singing on the radio, 'We are going
on a summer holiday ...' We've never been
on a summer holiday, or any holiday. She seems
to read my mind and turns up the volume
just as we turn left into Voortrekker Road.

'It's going to rain,' her first words
since we left Mitchells Plain.
I sense clouds forming but I see none.
She turns on the windscreen wipers
but there is no rain. It is her routine
so I do not question.

We turn into Gate 3 at Maitland Cemetery,
and I understand the windscreen wipers
and the silence and the summer holiday song
and the bucket. She has a routine here:
remove old flowers, insert fresh flowers,
pour fresh water, sweep away sand
and twigs and leaves. And then a short prayer.
She holds my hand. I try to hold my pain.
We're wiping our eyes, windscreen wipers.
We were sad and happy then. Sad
that he was gone. Not just happy

that he was out of his pain, but that we'd
be out of ours. But our pain remains.

We snake back along Jakes Gerwel Drive
in her silver Toyota with cowhide seats,
Cliff Richard singing, the sun shining.
We stop at McDonalds for a milkshake –
it is her routine, who am I to question ...

Published in *New Contrast*, Issue 178, 2017

AT SHREWBURY'S DINGLE

What is this place? I want to cartwheel
here, in this majestic garden that makes
my eyes smile and my spirit trampoline.
It is not my mother's little patch of green,
the allowance the poor get for our spirits
to crawl. It is a floral marching band with
trumpets and snare drums and cymbals.
I want to bring her here, to see this place,
many times the size of her kitchen table
but a fraction of its riches. We owe
such great debts to our mothers for their
burdens; we must do more than carry them
in our arms, on our backs, in our wombs.

I know these ancient trees have heard
death's cries, as have our mothers, but
know peace now. I should bring her here,
we should all bring our mothers here.

IN THE LANGEBERG MOUNTAINS

I know that I don't need to be here
to find words, I know
that I carry my songs with me,
my voice in my breast pocket.
So I am not looking for inspiration here
in this sea of mountains; gigantic waves paused,
holding their breath,
as though they've seen something so spectacular
that they dare not breathe.
'What did you see mountains?
what do you know?'

What draws man to such places
of ample sky
and distance of vision?
It can't be silence, for
there is no silence here.
The earth is never silent. Sound
echoes through every moment,
vibrating with life;
the wind whistles, and rustles the vines,
the sheep and donkey fill the air with their voices,
so do the chirping finches and the clapping locusts
and the creaking old trees. There is never silence
but also, there is never noise.

These are the sounds,
vibrations of life for which the spirit yearns;
here it can join the choir of life and be whole.
What man needs is not absolute silence
but silence from the noise he creates, in the world
and in his soul. Silence appeals to the mind
but life's sounds invigorates the spirit.

My trance is disturbed as the serenade is pierced
by the strong language of grape pickers (below
my mountain perch)
and the rattle of the tractor which carries their pickings,
('picking words from the vine of language,' I smile;)
stuttered yelping stabs across the valley, shrieks of laughter
then angry barking as unrefined as the grapes they pick.
'There is no silence here!' I frown.
Their dance is an ancient one –
an ancient rhythm to their taking from the earth
to give to man,
row by row, stanza by stanza
obedient to forms – sonnets, villanelles, pantoums.
This land blushes with centuries of their yelps and cackles,
their cries and menial joys. Their blood
seeps deep into the rich soil
and reddens the grapes they now pick.

Is this what the mountains hold secret?
Why are the mountains so silent
when everything else speaks,
or are we just not listening close enough?

Scores of centipedes wander blindly, directionless,
across the floor of our isolated cottage,
hoping to happen upon life.
They adorn our walls with their black length,
like one inch exclamation marks
or markings of a prisoner counting days till freedom.
Even they're not silent, they fall from walls onto hard tile –
'tick, tick' they pepper the air with their crash landings.

What do these Langeberg mountains know?
Why do they call us here?
Do they know our questions, our yearnings?
I must stop. And lie next to Bruno, the aging great dane
who has adopted me. He has peace in his tired eyes.
The pickers fade, earth's song dissolves,
all I hear is Bruno's heavy breathing.

Then the mountains speak.

They tell us that we know. That
we know what they know. That
we just need to listen. And
have courage to live in truth.

'So there is inspiration here after all,'
I hear Bruno say, causing me to instantly
leap to my feet in shock.
Talking mountains I can accept
but not talking dogs.

WE ASK

I have learned that we often
cannot understand –
an Eliot poem, a Dali painting,
the end of a loved one's breath –
that sometimes, all we can do is
walk through the winter mist
to the summer shine
that waits within.

RAINBOW

When we love,
our spirit reaches out to the other
like hands that clasp, then merge,
a new appendage, the two, one.

When the other goes,
that spirit-appendage remains
but bears a wound,
a wound that never heals,
an aching
like rain that never stops.

To have loved and lost
is to know this rain, this aching,
this pouring from a skyly lake
that never drains; the deeper
the love the vaster that lake,
the heavier the downpour.

But even in that rain,
that pouring, that aching,
a rainbow forms, the face
of the other, a reminder
that we have loved
and remain, hands clasping.

CRACKS

I am not afraid to speak
of pain, but most times
it is not I who voices pain
but pain itself that rumbles
through my throat and pen
and onto the page to alert
me to my cracks needing love.
And so I listen.

BLACKBIRD WANTING

His breathing is low, burdened
by the long, uphill walk. The blackbird
sees him. He knows why the blackbird
is there but has his doubts about
what to do.

The grey worms at the top of his head
have begun moving again. Rather than lie still
to do their work, the worms are moving,
as they occasionally do, more frequently
these days at the sun's earlier setting.
This is what the blackbird,
large and menacing, wants,
the worms. This is what he came to offer.

The blackbird, with its two-inch beak
throws open its wings to take flight.
It circles above where he is sitting
on a rickety old bench along a black
muddy path. Smaller and smaller circles
and then it dives. Suddenly,
he jumps to his feet, his breathing
crystal clear. The grey worms are lying still,
synapsing as they should,
floating in their magic and mystery.

He takes to the long walk home
without looking back, leaving
the blackbird wanting.

CHERYL AND I

Cheryl and I once sat on the roof
of her mother's house in Johannesburg.
It was the days of apartheid – white girls
were not to be sitting on rooftops with
black boys, not in this old mining town
in this hell, our brute luck to call home.
We just sat there, mute, Cheryl and I,
on the rooftop, coffee mugs in hand,
the thick smog holding our silence.

It made sense to me, sitting on a rooftop
in a place where nothing else made sense,
the silence a break from our hearts screaming.
Fed from birth with so much anger, we were,
stomachs distended with others' hatred that
we could not puke, rocks and lies pressed
deep into our guts, weighing down our youth.

She taught me to waltz and ride a motorbike,
us both screaming. We never kissed, but
we held hands, often. We danced and sped
and dreamed of a time when our stomachs
would empty and we'd both know silence.

She knows silence now, Cheryl, a silence
that leaves me empty, shouting on my own.
Sometimes, when I miss her, I sneak up
onto the roof of her mother's house,
coffee mug in hand, to sit there, with her.

In memory of my dear friend, *Cheryl McIntosh*
(1973 – 2003)

IF YOU SHOULD FALL

Where does it hurt?

With these arms
I hold you close
till my heartbeat
dissolves the hurt;
we become a song,
music that fills the holes
that mends the cracks
that nurtures the fallen tear drops
to new blossoms.

Where does it hurt?

I am there where it hurts,
there in your winter,
there with you,
there, till summer rises.

PASSAGE

I am the memory of every person
who fought for my freedom.

I am the echo
of every cry of despair,
of every chant of hope,
of every song of victory.

I am the dreams of my fathers.
I am their future. If I dream
from my lofty platform
like they dreamed
from their lowly basements
then what a great future it will be.

STILL STANDING

Still standing,
still breathing,
still angry.

Still growing,
still striving,
but still angry.

Though they shattered his innocence,
though they shook him cold,
though they put Apartheid's guns to his head
and punched their fists into his back,
he's still standing.

They've won
because he is still angry.
He's won
because he is still standing.

Published in *Heap of Stones*, Theart Press, 2009

WHERE TO LOOK

I appeared small when looking in their mirror
made of holy lies and frozen darkness that
choked the vein that carries love to hearts.
Not small like a child wanting to be an adult,
but small as in being something less – less
of a person, less of a man, less of me; more of
what they wanted me to be.

The reflection showed my face deformed,
my back hunched, arms and legs shrivelled,
the lights in my eyes faded, my flame doused.
In that mirror I had no name, everything
was dim, shrunken, small.

But, I had my own mirror.

ASKED TO INTRODUCE MYSELF

This I am, the mpingo tree, the sum of my memories
and dreams; I am the memories of my days and beyond –
sounds, textures sewn firmly into my seed; my days
like fingerprints on a cave wall, some crisp with joy,
some smudged by the blur of anger, the convulsion of pain.
I have felt the music of my spirit strummed at the peak
of my flesh; and known the long fall down narrow wells
endless with silent darkness.
                                This I am, the mpingo tree,
the dreams that my spirit sees, gardens in lands, rich
with aromas unchained, and dreams that flow in my veins,
with the songs of those hearts that beat before mine.
Dreams rise like mountains, summits calling, rivers gushing
across wonder lying on its back, arms outstretched, under
a dome lit by the whites of the eyes of other worlds peeping.
Each dream inviting a breath, a new sunrise.

I am the sum of my memories and my dreams,
that large ellipse that crosses borders and pierces
lines and circles and the simplicity of time and superstition;
the memories of gods' hands and men's fists and women's
caresses; dreams of my voice flowing through roots
to the earth, and my song rustling upon leaves to heaven.

I am the mpingo tree in an open plain without walls,
where the rabbit feeds on lush grasses, and the fox
feeds on the rabbit; where the incandescent orchestra
of spring is quietened by the lone cello of winter,
where orange and grey rise and fall on a Ferris wheel.

When I find silence, floating in that plain, I hear
endless memories and dreams, for I am an echo.
I am an echo of memories that vibrate to shake the fruit
from my branches, and dreams that glow like a sun
in each new leaf. I am a tree that will be chopped down
by men or sucked back into the earth by rot, but a tree
that once stood, like trees before and trees to come.
This I am, an echo, the mpingo tree, the sum
of my memories and dreams.

ONE FINITE LIFE

Short this life is, just one I've got,
finite in tenure whether I like it or not.

Death, is embracing fear, replacing dreams with 'I cannot,'
life, is taking a new step having a shot.

I will do the impossible, I will change the world,
I'll give hope to a despairing nation, I'll give bread to a starving girl;

I'll break all the records, I'll do what's never been done,
I'll give and know love, I'll be a billionaire of fun.

You can whip me with your words, you can bash me with your lies,
you can chain me to the ground with your rules, you can stab me with
your eyes;

I'll forgive all personal harm, I'll ignore all acts of mean,
but I will not forgive obstruction of my purpose and dream;

for I am a superman, I am a king,
I will not just lie down, I will get up and take to wing;

I will rise up as sure as the sun,
as sure as the springbok I will run,
as sure as the eagle I will fly
'cos I choose to live until I die.

What will you do with today, this hour, this minute?
Will you fill it with dull and fear or will you live it?

I will not tolerate any foe no matter weapon or munition,
especially if that foe is within me in the form of fear or
lack of ambition.

Short this life is, just one I've got,
finite in tenure whether I like it or not.
As sure as the eagle I will fly
'cos I choose, I choose to live, until I die.

Published in *Heap of Stones*, Theart Press, 2009

SKIPPING DINNER

'I do not eat meat,' caused every head in the bistro
to whip towards him with the wood and metal clang
of a trapdoor instantly inviting gravity to dinner.

Hooked by the back of his collar, he was prodded
to leave. To his left, a jeering crowd spat holy verses,
waved serving forks, stabbed steak knives into the air.

Some hurled beacons of civilisation. On his right,
a lamb blinked, nodded, a cow tilted her head.
'Beasts!' he thought, as he was sent to the gallows.

CONFESSION OF A
FORMER TEENAGE
DRUNK

I miss the warmth of drunkenness,
the safety of stupor, the prosperity,
the peace; for who has a care when
all the world sways in merriment?

I miss the soft joy, the brightness of
everything; how the drink soaks
into your muscles and bones making
you invincible, all-powerful, all-knowing.

I miss the lilting speech, the
philosophical slurring, the tall tales
that compensate for small lives,
the stories that no-one follows while
leaning against an old Ford Cortina
in the dead of night, doors open,
techno blaring, passing around a glass
of brandy and coke. I hated that drink,
brandy and coke, but liked how happy
it made me feel - home, unalone.

I miss how good it feels to embrace
a pal and grunt, 'I love you man,' bro, I
love you man,' confident
in your horsepower masculinity.

I miss the polony and chips gatsby
that sticks to your dry palate, that you
swallow without chewing in a race
to plug the holes in your stomach.

I miss the agony of holding back
projectiles of puke, swallowing, tasting
the acidic warning in the back of your molars,
juices announcing the inevitable.

I miss how everything eventually
slows down, becomes muffled;
the slowness of the fall, how your
knees slide along the concrete with
glee, the way the sidewalk feels
like rubber against your temple; how
the laughter grows the greater the pain.

I miss the mystery of time, the evaporation
of memory, how you move across miles
and hours effortlessly, miraculously,
defying the laws of physics, and society.

I miss the wildness and recklessness
of youth, of defying, trying, tasting. And
ultimately choosing.
A direction, a path.
To stay or go.

I left.
Gladly.
Perhaps,
I don't miss any of it after all.

THE MAN TO BE

The small man, stands between
the light and the wall; here he revels
in the deception of his large image,
but he is trapped, for when he looks
around, he is blinded by the light.

The great man, stands behind
the light, from where he can see
the contours of truth. His stature is not
determined by his reflection on a wall,
but by the expanse of his imagination.
He is free, for when he looks around, he
sees the vastness of the universe, whose
mysteries and beauties are his to explore.

Written for *Zachery Steinberg* on
the day of his bar mitzvah
16 February 2013

WHY NOT ME!

The little boy sat among cut up photos
of himself, strewn across the floor.
He had pasted cut-outs of his face
over the faces of people in magazines.

A disorder was declared – large words
for a little boy in a small world – caging him
with ignorance and special concoctions.

He had pasted his face onto the bodies of people
doing great things. Rather than his mind failing
his heart was dreaming, his spirit soaring.
'Why not me!' he determined, before another dose
was poured to reshape him and resize him
to the limits of how things have always been.

Graduation Day, Oxford University, 28 July 2017

MAKERS

This world of locked doors and dead-ends
is not ours, for we are free, endless. We
shake the rules to shape a world that boosts
the crops and fills the dams and cleans the air
that our children breathe as they walk through
doors flung wide. Our dreams hold the fuel
to keep the lights burning, the wheels turning,
hope churning. Tomorrow waits for us,
dreamers, those who dream with hearts
and hands, open, creating.

To create is to travel dark roads lit only
by our imagination. We face unknown
turns to unknown places but must go for we
are most alive when we are creating, and we
are most creative when traveling together.
We do not stand on the shoulders of giants,
we are lifted by the passion of fellow travellers,
and so we see further, climb higher.

We climb to the edge of mountaintops and lean
forward into wonder, unafraid, for there we find
the unseen, and so we walk and swim and fly,
for hope draws our feet into vast fields, deep
waters, infinite skies, rich with possibility.

DREAM CHILD

Dream child, dream;
see the garden that your soul knows,
that garden of majestic green trees,
of sun-filled fruit, of diamond waters.

Dream child, dream;
be the superhero you know you are;
that hero with endless strength,
in a timeless world, rich with possibility.

Dream child, dream;
fly into that moving picture,
that picture of tumbling laughter, of running
with arms waving, of rolling around, free.

And as you're flying free, soaring
to magical heavens, free,
free on your cloud-top perch,
thank the wind for its breath
and smile upon those who plucked
their wings to feather yours.

And keep being a child, child, be,
and keep living your dream, child, dream,
and keep being free, child, free.

ON THE OUTSIDE

Many live on the outside,
we know hunger and cold;

Broken promises keep us
on the outside, lies are told;

On the outside we struggle,
where hope is taken, sold;

But we will rise on the outside,
victory no longer on hold;

Inspired by greatness on the
outside, fierce and bold;

Wayde ran on the outside,
and he won gold!

TO A SEEKER

Don't stop at 'I don't know,' though this is
the first step, toward knowing. Seek to fill
your empty pockets with knowing. Burden
across the rocky terrain that compels, with
everything unexpected, enemy to the ankles
and spirit. Wrestle your way, in joy, to make
a path of beauty, that ends in a place that
leads to other places.

No human endeavour
could be greater. And no greater reward
exists than to reach that place, to peer
through the misty window in anticipation,

and to see yourself.

PRAYER

It hangs in mystery,
singing its songs
that light our paths at night.
'Look,' she says in wonder,
'the moon!'
'I see," he says,
looking into the eye of God.

SEEING, KNOWING

I didn't know what to look at;
the dripping woman who tempted my lips,
or the old man who tempted my dreams,
or the deep black that tempted my fear.

I rotated the photograph, this way,
then that, flipped it over, still
I didn't know what to look at;
like voyeuring a naked neighbour, undecided
about what to ogle the longest, or receiving
an anticipated letter, and not knowing
what to read first, or watching the evening
news, and not knowing when to stop crying.

And then I saw it –
the creator's fingerprint,
the photographer's breath,
and I could see no more,
only hear.

WHEN STRUMMED

It is a string my spirit, a taut string
that when strummed … sings, thunder,
my body gripped, swaying, quivering
like bright bolts in onyx skies, dancing
rainbow dust – toxins fall, light recall,
leaving me teary, goosebumped, panting.

SPIRIT WHISPERS

I

I don't know who to thank for this bliss.
I cannot explain the mystery of the flame
on my fingertips, at the edge of my spirit,
but I am grateful to be this alive.

II

An angel, like a winged-bull, comes ...
not a teacher, but a midwife,
to lift me up so that I can give birth
to beauty; beauty drawn from the spirit,
for only in this beauty is truth found.

I wake up from a death, a corpse
that knows only reason and logic,
to find my spirit waiting, neglected,
but willing to show me breath
and teach me light. And so I step out
of my silence, into my body's music,
and find that there I am not alone,
there is a circle of faces blowing
their breath upon me to help me
remember, to recognise myself.

I peek through the clouds,
just my head and neck emerge;
my head rotates casting my eyes
in wonder. Here my lungs feel most clear.
This is not a drug for short-term pleasure
but a temporary awakening. This
is where I go when I want to hear
the sunshine sing within me. This
is the closest to rapture that man can get –
here is no doubt, no uncertainty; this
is the purest man can be, the most
singular, the clearest. This
is the most perfect experience, for mangos
can have green patches, wine can be
corked,
clouds can cover the sun, but this
is a long sweet smoothness,
perfectly held in the universe's embrace,
with heaven's warmth.

III

We need so little, most times
all we need to fill our stomachs
are our memories and imagination.
There is beauty in this *memagination*
that makes odd-shaped things beautiful.
Our needs are small, for even a tiny flame
can light a palace. Our needs
are very simple;
but only when we are awake
do we know
that to surrender to the ecstasy
of our humanity,
the ecstasy of love,
the ecstasy of our senses,
the ecstasy of creative purpose,
is to live the fullness of the human experience.
Ecstasy is the spirit's best friend.
When the body leaves the spirit,
we stand in ecstasy.
Upon our death, our bodies are invested
in the earth to provide for future bodies,
just as our spirits return to the source
to provide for future spirits.
We are always holding hands.
All we need for peace is to awake
to the knowledge
that we are always holding hands.

IV

Our clutter flies and pierces our chests
like bullets and shrapnel; out of our backs
words fall, arranged in beauty. Our bodies
are filters, revealing wisdom.

The human experience is so finely poised
between darkness and light – that which
brings wisdom can also blind us, that which
brings ecstasy one moment, can drown us
in despair the next. But we know that
where there is joy, there is wisdom.

We can always choose to smile.

This is why, sometimes, our spirits just want to
be free and childlike, to laugh and run about
carelessly with our arms waving wildly in the
warm afternoon wind. Man's obsession
with knowledge will rid him of pleasures.
When we deconstruct joy we no longer
have joy, and so never know wisdom.
Some mysteries must remain mysteries.

V

Beware,
our eyes are most easily deceived.
Just the wave of a magician's wand
fools our eyes into impossibilities.
We in turn are fooled by the lies
that our eyes accept. We should know
that truth cannot be seen by the eye,
it is only seen by the spirit.
We need to quieten the flesh,
to hear the whisper of the spirit,
like the whisper,
not of the ocean's waves,
but of its vibrations.
The noise of haste
distorts whispered wisdom,
leaving our spirits parched. The well is dry
when we merely think and feel, but overflows
when we listen with our spirits' ears.
Can the spirit refuse to speak,
leaving us dumb in our silence?
Or is the spirit always speaking
but we are too distracted to hear?
We need unspectacular moments,
like the darkness needed for stars to shine.
Only during winter, in the absence of foliage,
do we see the beauty of a tree's structure.

We need to spend more time listening
than worrying about not being able to hear.
We can open or close our mouths,
and so choose to speak or be silent.
We can open or close our eyes,
and so can choose to see or not.
But we cannot open or close our ears,
they are always open, always available
to hear, already ready to listen. This
is our most important faculty.

VI

How does the fruit tree
spread the magic of its seed? It produces
a sweet fruit to be picked and consumed,
the seed invested in the earth. The fruit
has to be taken for wisdom and magic to grow.
Our dreams are the fruit, they have to be
picked and eaten. We have to walk our path,
we have to fly to be alive. We should
learn from seagulls that have discovered
when they tap their feet on the soil,
earthworms emerge, providing a meal.
Sometimes we need to tap
on the surface of impossibility
to bring dreams to reality.

We have to speak to the mountain,
store our wisdom there, and listen
to the mountain to hear wisdom
of those before. We can never predict
what we will hear or whether we will hear
anything at all, but we must listen.
Tap the mountain lightly with your palms
like the footsteps of a mountain leopard,
to awaken the voices. I hear these voices
in my flesh; there are taste buds
all over my body
that sing delightful sweet melodies.

VII

Shout with joy – no words, just the sounds
of our spirits quivering in delight; sprinkle
each breath with glitter of sound to see
our spirits' joy as we hear it sing.

Published in *New Orleans Review*, Issue 43, 2017

From 2012 to 2014, at least once a week, I entered into self-induced deep meditations, brief trances that lasted only a few seconds. Upon emerging from the trances, I would concentrate on any received ideas or images and record these immediately. I call this process, 'peak listening.' This poem has been crafted over this three-year period from ideas and images that emerged while peak listening.

BEFORE SLEEP

I lay in bed soaked in softness – pillow
cradling by hard plans that bow down
as I stare at the white ceiling up there
in the distance, the silence that sneaks in,
drawing a smile in that nowhere place
we all know but forget. I lay there
for my allotment of blinks before sleep

listening closely to the silence, I hear
memories, see them, tiny characters
dancing and tumbling through my veins,
standing on cells stacked like a stage,
performing animated scenes from dramas
that tell stories of people walking on air
and holding their breath for days, and
holding fire in their hands, and a party
of giants awake to that nowhere place
that smiles and sings, awake to
heartbeats, to music, to softness.

'Are you still awake?' I hear her ask,
poking me in the side, startling me back.
'Yip,' I say, smiling, 'just dreaming.'
'Dreaming while awake?' she frowns.
'The best time,' I say, reaching over
to kiss her, and turn off the light.

IN THE CHOIR

I step into moving traffic; am struck
by yesterdays. I want to look ahead
but they call to me, 'it is not wrong
to look back a time while going forward.'
Their words release the songs confined
to my cells; in my hands, I hold stones
that hold their heartbeats. We're flowing,
I am home, magnificent.

BUTTERFLIES

We've waited all winter
to open these garden gates,
to step out of grey coats
and into the era of spring,
rearranged as supermen,
unafraid to breathe, stronger
to fight shrinkage, stronger
to hold each other's hands.

THESE WORDS

All I have is these words that pour
from this scruffy bag in my chest,
like the scruffy bag that pours
the skinny bones of an infant corpse,
starved, of hope.

Words trickle down the wrinkled cheeks
of a defeated mother who knows
too much sun and too much sin
and too much sorrow. She knows
the rhythm of my words, these words,
this mother, who cries the cry of the desert,
that cry long after the tears, long after
the stench, long after the stones are piled
in random heaps to remember
the organised culling of her meaning.
Word after word, bullet after bullet,
lie after … promise, her tree goes silent,
her mountain mute.

All I have is these words,
no bite of bread
or drop of drink
or bomb to blast
or gun to shoot
to take her eye, for his eye, or my eye,
but I,

I have are these words, these
pockets of power upon my lips,
lips of limit
but spirit ten thousand suns bright,
words that reach high into the sky
to catch bullets in flight,
words that dig deep into the darkness
of hatred to bring light,
words that soak into the soul in pain
to bring warmness at night,

words that makes those who do wrong
turn to do what is right,
words that makes those with selfish blindness
awake and have sight,
words that awakens the songs of dignity
and silences power and might,
words that brings water from sand in delight,
words that make old enemies turn and unite,
words that dissolves the lies
of us and them, black and white.

All I have is these words
but these words walk on water,
these words dance across waterfalls
and push back the clouds
to bring the sun back into view
and pushes down the sea levels
and raises the crop from its slumber
in rich soil, and raises the fallen school,
and fallen bridge
and fallen people
with their fallen hope.

All I have is these words
that leap from these lips
that pulse with every living beat,
that beat, heartbeat that makes us one.
When that mother cries
we all cry,
for being one is all our spirits know.

All I have is these words
that I now offer to you,
because all we have
is each other.

THE STORY OF BOHMN

His back pressed hard against the white wall
that towered over him like a tsunami
of solid marble, a colossal headstone
that revealed his round brown face, bright
against the cold whiteness. Ballakisten's head, heels,
trembling hands, pressed as deep into that wall
as his fear could muster.

                It thundered toward him,
the enormous fighter bull the size of morbid darkness,
horns of solid anger, who for eight hundred years
had violently been executing evil men's justice.
It rushed like a hurricane – rocks and trees and
horror flung into the air. Its hooves pounded
the red dry earth showering the boy with a terror
so deep and so sharp that it awoke fears that lay
dormant within him for centuries.

                In flight the bull arranged
its horns to ensure both pierced the hapless life;
lowering its head, it thrust its twin spears forward
with contemptuous force. Like a fierce wrecking
ball it lunged at Ballakisten, son of slaves.

The boy's eyes remained tightly shut in this,
his final moment. He heard the groans and cries
of his forebears pounding in his chest. In his silence
he could hear their songs racing through his veins,
the sad songs, the freedom songs that his grandfathers
and great-grandmothers had sung in the belly of a beast.

The sharpened tip of the bull's horn bore down
on the boy's forehead. In the instant before the mystery
and misery of death, the Judge held up her scepter
and the bull froze. Frozen, it hung, suspended in the air.
From a distance it appeared as though the bull had pierced
the boy's frame and lodged its horns into the marble wall;
a whirlwind of shrieks and cheers erupted from the arena.

But untouched, the boy slowly opened his teary eyes
to the shock of the enormous killer staring angrily at him.
He gasped, fresh air into decaying lungs, and immediately
shut his eyes and winced, repeating the prayer that he had
been repeating ever since his sentence for trying to run
from his inherited hell: 'Let light shine upon my wretched
soul.' Again he opened his eyes, more tentatively, more
confused, wondering if this was his first experience of the
afterlife. His eyes scanned wildly as eyes do when chaos
breathes. The stench of the bull's breath burned in his
nostrils; its muzzle, still wet with rage, was at his chest.
He remained pressed against the wall, drained
of movement, of comprehension, swollen with fear.

'I will give you one chance,' the Judge spoke, her melodic
voice singing around the arena, 'Time to perform one act,
one supreme act of love.' The Judge reached up, reached deep
into the sky and withdrew a flaming star from the universe.
She placed the flaming ball on a column of light and spun it.
'When this star stops spinning, your time will be up
and you will find yourself in this exact position.' The boy
did not stir. 'If your act of love is indeed supreme and
pleases me, you will be released, and be free to roam
the earth and the heavens forever. If your act displeases me,
your fate will be sealed. Now go!'

He had never been beyond the city walls, but now Ballakisten
was released into the great unknown, alone, the Judge's words,
'A supreme act of love,' throbbing in his memory. Unknown,
this terrain, his task, and its tenure. Unknown, this slave boy
from unknown transplanted seed.

Men with ideas ambushed him, 'Build a monument to the Judge,'
'Plant a tree that will never die, that will feed us for all eternity.'
Forty-four days he wandered, crowds following him, spitting
advice but still no supreme act of love. Anxiety swelled
as time passed with the spinning of the flaming star. Until
he walked in silence,
and was able to listen,
to see. Light,

like lukewarm mist flowed over him and through him, and lit his
spirit. Flames towered and waved their arms, and kicked up dust
with their feet in dance. In the flames an old bent woman dug
with her hands into the earth and handed him a scroll.
The text was feint, the font foreign, but he understood:

> *show love to your tormented tormenter*
> *let your spirit be your tormenter's wings*
> *free yourself*
> *and Bohmn will be*

As the flames of the spinning star drew still, the flames of the
boy's spirit began to lie down. He smiled, for the first time
in his years, he smiled like no slave boy has ever smiled, for
suddenly he knew.
He knew!
He knew his supreme act of love for there is a knowing
that comes when we hear our spirits speak.

The star stopped its spin and Ballakisten, son of slaves,
returned with his back pressed firm against the cold hard
towering white marble wall with the killer bull frozen
only fractions before him. His fear, like compost, fed
his love, a blossom that now glowed within him. His spirit
sang with a voice like rustling leaves, like ocean waves
running their hands over pebbled beaches. His heart beat
with the rhythm of the seas, his muscles danced
to the dance of the seasons, the earth's lungs were his lungs,
the earth's light was his light, 'I am the earth,' he smiled,
and began to speak:

'When we listen, there is a knowing
to be found that helps us see.
There is a knowing to be found
when we look with love into the eyes
of anger, of hatred. We find freedom there,
freedom that rises above all city walls,
above judgement; freedom that silences
ancient cries, calms ancient storms.
Only love can set the fearful free.'

The boy opened his arms
as if to embrace the ancient killer.
He looked into the bull's eyes; looked deep
into its eyes, with love and saw himself there.
The bull understood. It saw a river of green light
flow with purpose that it had never seen
in its eight hundred years, and rise
through the boy's feet, upwards, feeding his flame
and then spread, till it filled his every part
and pulsated beyond his limits. In the light
the bull could see fish from the sea, apples
from a tree, clouds of the sky, grass of the plains.

The arena crowd rose in voice, rose to their feet,
his doom their delight for they had not seen any act,
any act of supreme love. 'Your time is up!'
the Judge declared. She lowered her scepter
and immediately the bull continued on its deadly path.

The crowd filled the arena with their cheers.
The enormous thick white marble wall crumbled
as the bull crashed forward. Everyone gasped
as one gasps when your spirit walks that tightrope
between horror and delight. The earth convulsed,
the arena shook with volcanic vigor, cosmic birth.
The city walls cracked. Everything stopped. Silence
descended on the arena, on the city, as white dust
and red dust rose in a plume like a final breath.

From the heap of stones, rubble, a being emerged,
a never-before-seen spectacular being in the form
of a majestic winged bull, the color of marble,
physique of a fighter bull and wings of a harpy eagle.
The flap of its wings sang with a thousand voices.
Around the arena it flew, to rapturous applause
from the crowd, newly converted, for they knew.
'Bohmn! Bohmn!' the crowd chanted.
'Bohmn,' the Judge smiled, for she knew,
as the crowd knew, as the boy had come to know.

And then Bohmn, the bull with wings
of that slave boy's spirit, the god
of love that leads to freedom, flew off.

Bohmn can be seen flying across the sky
if you listen closely. It is known to those
who seek love, love that leads to freedom.

ABOUT THE AUTHOR

Dr. Athol Williams is a poet and social philosopher from Cape Town, South Africa.

He has published six books of poetry and his poems have been published in literary journals in South Africa (New Contrast, New Coin, Stanzas), the UK (Popshot, Clare Market Review, Inky Needles), the USA (New Orleans Review, The Perch, Poetry Quarterly), France (Those That This) and Sweden (Stark).

He has read his poetry at literary festivals in South Africa (McGregor, Lowveld, SANAA, Open Book, Kimberley, Off the Wall, UNISA Poetry Sessions), the UK (Chipping Campden, Aspects) and France (Poets Live).

Athol has twice been awarded the Sol Plaatje European Union Poetry Award, won the Parallel Universe Poetry Competition at Oxford University, and been shortlisted for the South African Literary Award for poetry.

He holds seven degrees from Oxford, Harvard, MIT, London School of Economics, London Business School and Wits.

www.atholwilliams.com

www.ingramcontent.com/pod-product-compliance
Lightning Source LLC
Chambersburg PA
CBHW031538040426
42445CB00010B/603